If perticuliar care and attention is not paid to the Ladies we are determined to foment a Rebellion, and will

(left margin, vertical) Learning is not attained by chance, it must be sought for with ardour — Great necessities call out great virtues

(right margin, vertical) not hold ourselves bound by any Laws in which we have no voice, or Representation. Do not put such unlimited power into the hands of the Husbands Remember all Men would be tyrants if they could —

The affection I feel for my Friend is of the tenderest kind, matured by years, sanctified by choise and approved by Heaven. Angles can witness to it's purity, wha care I then fa the Ridicule of Britains should this testimony of it fall into their Hands— known only to his own Heart, is the conflict it has cost me— I wish a thousen How lonely are my days? How soli any national prejudices they ashamed to oun I ever posessed every one who Manifests a regad Absent Friend. — I am not America capable of anything, she vigou.~ My whole Soul is absorpt est Friend. the welfare and happi ages yet unborn, depend for their and skillfull the Honest and up— committed to him. It would not of my Heart upon this occasion. How much is compromised fondly can I call you mine, consecrates the most imit— erated by a cruel destiny, sometimes too sensibly fa times when the heart is er impre ssions, or is over- comfortable tha I feel world! care fo ing hard tha sou cooler the repin- me bless the my comforts active resolut- ed in a More Nature, he can

matured by years, sanctified by choise and approved by Heaven. sacrifice I have made and the con- times I had gone with him.— tary are my Nights? If I ever had are done away and I am of so narrow a spirit ~ I loe or shew an attachment to my elated or depressd. I know undertakes with spirit and in the Idea. The honour of my dear- nens of this wide extended Country, happiness and security upon the able right discharge of the important trust become me to write the free flow My Dearest Friend in tha short sentance? How bound by every tie which able Friendship, yet sep- I feel the pangs of absence my own repose. There are peculiarly awake to ten when philosophy slumbers, parried by sentiment more to Nature. It is then. myself alone in the wide without any one to tenderly me, or lend me an assist- through the difficulties round me, yet my reason disaproofs eing thaught and bids hand from whence flow. "Man and bad is fashion- different mould." independent ley scarcly realize all

those which blind our see to his. As it not natural to suppose that as our dependance is greater, on attachment is stronger? I find in my own breast a sympathetic pain always op- nating upon the near approach of Letters from my dear Absent Friend. I cannot determine the exact distance when this secret charm begins to operate.

To the "grown-ups" who read to me as a child, especially my parents, Hale and Lindy Boggs.
To the grown-ups I once read to, especially my son and daughter, Lee and Rebecca Roberts.
To the children I continue to read to, especially my grandchildren.
And in memory of my dear friend Eden Ross Lipson,
who knew more than anyone about children's books.

—Cokie

For David and Peter,
Ever thine

—Diane

Resources used by the artist when transcribing excerpts from the
original historical documents referenced in the endpapers:

The Library of Congress, Women's History
http://memory.loc.gov/ammem/index.html

Massachusetts Historical Society, Correspondence between John and Abigail Adams
http://www.masshist.org/digitaladams/aea/index.html

Founding Mothers: Remembering the Ladies. Text copyright © 2014 by Cokie Roberts. Illustrations copyright © 2014 by Diane Goode. All rights reserved. Manufactured in China.
No part of this book may be used or reproduced in any manner whatsoever without written permission except in the case of brief quotations embodied in critical articles and reviews.
For information address HarperCollins Children's Books, a division of HarperCollins Publishers, 10 East 53rd Street, New York, NY 10022. www.harpercollinschildrens.com

Library of Congress Control Number: 2013936887   ISBN 978-0-06-078002-9 (trade bdg.) — ISBN 978-0-06-078003-6 (lib. bdg.)

Typography by Dana Fritts 13 14 15 16 17 SCP   10 9 8 7 6 5 4 3 2 1 ❖ First Edition

COKIE ROBERTS

FOUNDING MOTHERS

Remembering the Ladies

Illustrated by DIANE GOODE

HARPER

An Imprint of HarperCollinsPublishers

Dearest friend

LETTER OF INTRODUCTION

*W*HEN I WAS IN SCHOOL, *I learned a lot about the men we call the Founding Fathers—George Washington, Thomas Jefferson, Benjamin Franklin, and others. But aside from a story about Martha Washington spending a freezing winter at Valley Forge with the American army during the Revolutionary War, I don't remember ever being taught anything about the women who lived at the time the thirteen American colonies decided to break from Britain and build a country. I knew nothing of the mothers, wives, sisters, daughters, and female friends of the men who wrote the Declaration of Independence, fought in the revolution, created the Constitution, and formed our first government. I would have read books about the women if they had been available. History always interested me, and of course reading about women made tales from the past more real to me.*

My interest in history led me to my job as a news reporter writing about politics and government. To do my job well, I needed to understand better what the men who wrote our country's charters were thinking when they crafted those documents. As I learned more about the men, I wondered more about the women. What were they doing while their husbands, sons, brothers, friends, and fathers were off serving the country? I suspected that they had wonderful stories to tell if I could only hear them. And now I know they did.

The way we learn about the past is through letters and diaries, plus books written in earlier times and objects like clothes and cooking tools that tell us what people wore and how they lived. The Founding Fathers wrote hundreds of letters and articles that have been preserved and published over the centuries. But because women weren't considered important, their letters were often destroyed or stuffed in a box somewhere and lost for years. But I was able to find enough traces of our country's female forebears to piece together their very interesting lives.

Some women went off to war with the men; some served as spies; some wrote political poems and plays; some ran businesses and farms; many lived very difficult lives as the men were gone for months, sometimes years at a time. The eight long years of the Revolutionary War required many women to show incredible bravery in the face of danger to themselves and their children. By keeping everything together on the home front, the women made it possible for the men to go off to battle, or to congress, or on diplomatic missions. Without the women doing what they did, it would have been very hard for the men to "found" a nation. That's why I call them the Founding Mothers, and I know you will enjoy getting to know them.

These women were feisty and funny and flirty. And they were great Patriots—completely devoted to the American cause. As the British general Lord Cornwallis wrote during the war, "We may destroy all the men in America, and we shall still have all we can do to defeat the women."

Cokie Roberts

Women Through the Years

1765 The British pass the Stamp Act, taxing many things the Americans need, like paper. The Americans start protesting against British rule. The protesters include women who write poems, plays, and pamphlets attacking the "mother country."

1774 Deborah Franklin dies after running all of Benjamin Franklin's businesses and the postal service. Benjamin comes home from England, where he had been living since 1757.

1775 The British attack Lexington and Concord, starting the American Revolution. Martha Washington and other officers' wives join the army camp in Massachusetts. Other women go to war with their husbands.

1787–1788 The states adopt the Constitution, setting up the executive, legislative, and judicial branches of government.

1789 George Washington takes office as the first president under the new Constitution, and Martha Washington goes to the temporary capital of New York as the first First Lady.

1800 The government moves to the brand-new capital city of Washington, and the second First Lady, Abigail Adams, moves into the unfinished White House.

1801 Thomas Jefferson becomes president and appoints James Madison as secretary of state. Dolley Madison begins to throw big Washington parties.

1776 The Continental Congress passes the Declaration of Independence, claiming that America should be a separate country from Great Britain. Abigail Adams writes that the new country should "remember the ladies."

1778 The American army freezes at Valley Forge. Martha Washington and Caty Greene try to cheer up the troops.

1780 American women, spurred on by Esther Reed's "Sentiments of an American Woman," raise money for the troops. The fundraiser helps morale.

1783 A peace treaty with Great Britain ends the war, and America is officially a free nation. Sally Jay is with her husband in Paris when he signs the treaty.

1809 James Madison takes office as the fourth president, and Dolley is a very popular and powerful First Lady.

1812 A second war with Britain is declared because the English are interfering with America's ships sailing across the Atlantic Ocean.

1814 The British invade Washington. Dolley Madison saves the portrait of George Washington from destruction by enemy troops.

1815 A peace treaty officially ends the war. America and Great Britain never fight each other again.

ELIZA LUCAS PINCKNEY

Eliza. Pinckney

ELIZA LUCAS WAS ONLY SIXTEEN YEARS OLD WHEN **HER** father went off to fight for England against Spain and left her in charge of three plantations in South Carolina. On the plantations—or big farms—slaves did most of the work planting and harvesting rice. Eliza thought it was silly just to grow rice and nothing else—she thought her plantations should grow indigo—a plant used for making blue dye.

Many of the soldiers' uniforms in Europe were blue, so the armies needed indigo and Eliza was convinced she could make it grow. All of the experienced farmers laughed at her and told her she could never make it work—but they were wrong. After several years of trying and failing, she finally succeeded and indigo became the biggest money-making crop in South Carolina before the American Revolution, and a nineteen-year-old girl had made that happen.

Eliza married Charles Pinckney, another plantation owner, and they soon had three children. When the Revolutionary War broke out, the Pinckneys were staunch American Patriots. Both of Eliza's sons were taken prisoner by the British, and after they were released they fought with General George Washington. The British also ransacked and ruined Eliza's home and left her with no crops and no money.

After the war, she lived at her daughter Harriott's plantation and helped run it. Our first president, George Washington, traveled to South Carolina while he was in office. There he made a special trip to see Eliza Pinckney and her daughter Harriott. And when Eliza died, Washington insisted on honoring her at her funeral for the service she had given to the country.

ELIZA was always thinking up ideas for making money on her plantations—what she called her "little schemes." She cultivated figs to dry and sell, and she planted oak trees, certain that one day the colonies would need wood for ships. She raised silkworms and put the women and girls to work making silk. Her family has saved one of the silk dresses they made and now, more than two hundred fifty years later, museums around the country put it on display.

Indigo ~ South Carolina

Even though she was very young, Eliza had been well educated in England. She set up a school for the slaves on her plantations and taught her little sister as well. She even acted as a lawyer for some of the local people, writing wills for them. And she kept studying herself—reading every book in English or French that she could find.

DEBORAH READ FRANKLIN

THOUGH DEBORAH READ AND BENJAMIN FRANKLIN MET in Philadelphia when they were teenagers, Ben soon went off to England. Years later they got back together and Deborah's mother let Ben open a printing shop in the back of her own variety store. Deborah worked in both shops, quickly becoming an accomplished businesswoman.

Ben started writing a newspaper and experimenting with inventions, and grew so well known that he was called to public service. Deborah worked to expand the printing enterprise into a series of shops along what was then the frontier—western Pennsylvania. And when Ben accepted the title of postmaster, it was Deborah who ran the postal service.

She had to take charge because Ben was out of the country for years at a time. He represented the Pennsylvania colony in England and thought it important for him to stay there to argue against laws like the Stamp Act that the Americans thought were unfair. Deborah was left to run everything, and Ben thought she did an excellent job of managing money, saying she was "a fortune" to him. But she missed him and wanted him home. Though she begged him to come back, Ben didn't return to America until after Deborah died. Many years later he had a dream that he met his wife in heaven and tried to renew the marriage. But in the dream Deborah wouldn't have him, telling him that she had been his wife for almost fifty years: "Be content with that."

"I had not given offence to any person at all~ but if anyone come to disturb me, I would show them proper resentment."

$\mathscr{B}$EN was in England when the hated Stamp Act became law, and his Philadelphia neighbors thought he hadn't fought hard enough against it. Furious, they decided to tear down his house. Instead of hiding, Deborah asked a couple of relatives to bring guns, and when the angry mob arrived she scared away the crowd. When Ben heard the story he praised her "spirit and courage." But he still didn't come home like Deborah wanted him to do.

After Ben was named first postmaster general for the colonies, Deborah was left to make sure the mail was delivered. When Lord Loudon, the Englishman in charge of the postal service, tried to fire one of her workers, Deborah stood up to him—accusing his men of treating her "very unpolitely" and complaining that he was slowing down the mail system. So much for Lord Loudon.

MERCY OTIS WARREN

M Warren

At the time of the American Revolution, of course there were no radios, televisions, or computers. So politicians depended on newspapers and pamphlets to spread their messages. One of the most important writers arguing for independence from Britain was Mercy Otis Warren.

It was unusual for a woman to have such a powerful voice, but Mercy was an unusual woman. Her father, brother, and husband were all prominent in Massachusetts politics, and they listened to what Mercy had to say. She enjoyed a better education than most girls of her time—studying along with her brothers until they went to college, which girls weren't allowed to do.

The Patriots—men plotting to free the colonies from the British—met at Mercy Warren's home and encouraged her to write plays and poems attacking the governor of Massachusetts, who was loyal to the English king. Theater performances were against the law at the time! The people who read the plays in the newspapers of Boston, New York, and Philadelphia realized the British weren't treating the Americans fairly.

After fighting began in Massachusetts, Mercy wrote to the congressmen meeting in Philadelphia, who were trying to decide whether to declare independence. Her letters describing how British warships threatened Boston and how enemy soldiers destroyed churches and occupied the city shocked the Congress.

Because Americans were rebelling against their laws, the British decided to stage a surprise attack. English soldiers marched on Concord, Massachusetts, where they planned to kidnap Patriots and then go to Lexington to destroy the rebels' supplies. But the Americans found out about the plan and put up a fight. The British won the battles but lost many soldiers. Mercy Warren wrote about the battles to men in Congress and helped convince them to send an army to Massachusetts.

George Washington headed the American troops sent to Cambridge, Massachusetts, to battle the British in Boston. Mercy went to meet him and the other generals and wrote to John Adams about it. She thought Washington was "amiable and accomplished" . . . but General Charles Lee? Though she found him "sensible" and "judicious," she also thought he was marked by "ugliness" and "unpoliteness." She didn't know we'd be reading her letters more than two hundred years later!

WOMEN WRITERS

THOUGH WOMEN COULDN'T RUN FOR OFFICE or speak before large crowds at the time of the American Revolution, they *could* write—they could put quill to parchment in the privacy of their homes. And several of them, like Mercy Otis Warren, wrote political poems and plays, hoping to shape history. Usually they published their writings under fictitious names; many of the men did that too. (Often everyone knew who they were anyway!) But during the war, when women had to take on much of the work of their absent husbands, brothers, fathers, or sons, some writers grew bolder. They started signing their own names to their works. And their writing turned to subjects like women's education, women's problems, and even women's rights.

LETTERS

Women's private writings—letters and diaries—tell us much more about their lives than anything published for the public. Reading their mail (it's okay to be nosy—they've been dead for a long time!) you learn what women were happy about and worrying about along with everyday happenings like who was having babies and what was the latest fashion. Unfortunately, because women weren't considered important, most of their letters were destroyed. Thank goodness we have the ones we do!

"REMEMBER THE LADIES"

One of the most famous letters ever written was from Abigail to her husband, John Adams. With independence from Britain, she realized America would need another form of government. "In the new Code of Laws," Abigail advised, the Congress should "remember the ladies"; otherwise, she warned, "we are determined to foment a rebellion." John laughed at her, but Abigail's "remember the ladies" has echoed through our history.

MAKING THE CASE AGAINST ENGLAND

Women writers like Annis Boudinot Stockton wrote poems that angered the public against the British. Here are a few lines of her poem rallying the Patriots after the Battle of Bunker Hill, where American General Joseph Warren was killed:

Thousands of heroes from his dust shall rise;

Who still shall freedom's injur'd cause maintain,

And show the lawless king the rights of men.

MAKING THE CASE FOR WOMEN

Though few Americans considered men and women as equals, some female writers bravely argued for women's rights. Best known was Judith Sargent Murray, who shocked readers with her magazine article "On the Equality of the Sexes" but also made them think about the subject. A couple of years later, when Englishwoman Mary Wollstonecraft's *Vindication of the Rights of Women* arrived in America, everybody rushed to read it.

AMERICA'S FIRST BESTSELLER

It was the bestselling book in the country for decades, and it was about a woman wronged by a man. The publisher of the sad story of *Charlotte Temple* by Susanna Rowson told the author that "sales exceed those of any of the most celebrated novels." The book is still in print.

PHILLIS WHEATLEY

Phillis Wheatley

WHILE GEORGE WASHINGTON WAS CAMPED IN Cambridge, he invited a truly remarkable woman to pay him a visit. Phillis Wheatley had been raised as a slave, but by the time she met General Washington she was an internationally celebrated poet.

No one knew how old the little girl was when she was snatched from her parents in Africa and stashed aboard the slave ship *Phillis*, but the Wheatleys guessed she was probably seven or eight because she still had some of her baby teeth. Susannah Wheatley, the mother of the family, bought Phillis to help her with household chores.

Soon eighteen-year-old Mary Wheatley, who taught Phillis English and Bible studies, realized how smart her student was, and by age twelve Phillis was writing poetry and living more like a family member than a servant. Eventually the Wheatleys freed her.

When newspapers printed her poems, no one could believe that a young slave was the author; people were even more amazed when a book of her poetry was published in England. After General Washington read Phillis's poem praising him, he wrote to her saying he wanted to meet someone "so favored by the muses."

It might surprise you that Phillis Wheatley lived in Boston, since we think of slavery as Southern. But before the Revolution, slavery was legal in all of the American colonies. Many slaves suffered under harsh conditions and few enjoyed the treatment Phillis received. Another Massachusetts slave, Elizabeth Freeman—called Mumbet—won her freedom in a lawsuit against her owners that helped lead to the abolition of slavery in the state.

Here's one of Phillis Wheatley's poems where she wrote about slavery as the reason she so loved freedom:

Whence flow these wishes for the common good,

By feeling hearts alone best understood,

I, young in life, by seeming cruel fate

Was snatched from Afric's fancied happy seat:

What pangs excruciating must molest,

What sorrow labor in my parents' breast.

ABIGAIL ADAMS

Abigail Adams

"YOU ARE REALLY BRAVE, MY DEAR, YOU ARE AN HEROINE," wrote John Adams to his wife, Abigail. The man who would become our second president was then at the Continental Congress in Philadelphia while his wife and four children were home in Massachusetts in daily danger from the British.

Abigail strongly believed in American independence, so supported her husband's political activities, but she had to keep the farm going by herself, always worrying where the British would strike next. John wrote that if it got really dangerous she should "fly to the woods with our children." Think how alone she must have felt!

Abigail, who sent John constant advice about the new government and current updates about politics, kept her letters coming when he went to Europe on diplomatic missions. Finally, after he had been gone for six years, she joined John in England.

In the first nationwide election, John Adams won as George Washington's vice president. Abigail moved to New York, the temporary capital city, and then to Philadelphia, where she assumed the job of First Lady once John was elected president. Then it was on to the brand-new city of Washington and the unfinished White House, which was so cold it took fires in thirteen chimneys to keep it warm.

John lost reelection to Thomas Jefferson, and the Adams couple retired to Massachusetts. Abigail lived to see her son, John Quincy Adams, become secretary of state, but she died before he was elected as the country's sixth president.

After he grew up, John Quincy Adams described the terrifying time of the Revolution in Massachusetts: "For the space of twelve months my mother with her infant children dwelt, liable every hour of the day and night to be butchered in cold blood, or taken and carried to Boston as hostages." But at the time Abigail bravely wrote, "Danger they say makes people valiant."

When Abigail advised John to "remember the ladies," she was eager to improve the lives of American women. She was especially interested in education, feeling that too many women were deprived of decent schooling. Even though she and her sisters had been taught well by their preacher father and his students, Abigail never thought her education was good enough. After the Revolution many women's schools were established so that educated mothers could raise sons to be good citizens.

MARTHA WASHINGTON

Martha Washington

"I NEVER IN MY LIFE KNEW A WOMAN SO BUSY FROM EARLY morning until late at night as was Lady Washington." That's what a visitor to Valley Forge wrote. It was a miserable winter at the army camp, and the freezing, starving troops threatened to leave their posts if conditions didn't improve. Martha Washington helped convince them to stay by sewing for the soldiers, cooking for them, nursing them, praying with them, and joining the other officers' wives to entertain them. The troops loved her.

Martha spent every winter of the eight long years of war at military camps with General George Washington. It was uncomfortable and often dangerous, but she did it because her husband needed her to help keep the soldiers from deserting.

After the war was finally over, Martha hoped to live quietly at home in Virginia. But George's many admirers came to visit. One year 423 people came to Mount Vernon, the Washington home, and Martha had to make sure they all had meals and beds. And she and George had adopted her two young grandchildren, who also needed her attention.

When Washington was elected as the first president, it was up to his wife to figure out the job of first First Lady. Every week she gave a party where anyone who was dressed nicely could attend. She had so much to do and so little fun that she complained, "I think I am more like a state prisoner than anything else."

Early in the war, Martha admitted: "I shudder every time I hear the sound of a gun." But still she bravely went to camp. Even more bravely, she volunteered for the inoculation against smallpox. A lot of people died from it. But if they survived, they usually didn't get the disease, which was killing thousands of Americans. Martha's example helped the troops accept Washington's order that they take the treatment. If the soldiers had not been protected against smallpox, America might have lost the war.

Winter at Valley Forge

In the summers at Mount Vernon, Martha directed the slaves to make provisions for the troops. They would spin wool from the sheep and weave it into cloth; they would preserve fruits and vegetables for the next winter. When Martha's carriage full of the fresh supplies pulled into camp, the soldiers cheered: "Lady Washington is here!" Those supplies were just some of the many contributions African Americans made to the revolutionary cause.

WOMEN WARRIORS

WHEN MEN WENT OFF TO WAR, often their wives and children went along as well. Usually these "camp followers" were too poor to be able to live at home without a man to do paid work because there weren't many jobs for women then. The women worked for the army—they cooked and washed and sewed, and they received a small salary. They also helped keep the weapons in working order by doing things like watering the cannons. Sometimes they even took over the big guns after their husbands were wounded.

Some women disguised themselves as men and fought alongside the other soldiers. Other women served as spies and messengers. When enemy soldiers asked for information about American troops, many women bravely refused to cooperate.

SOLDIER

Deborah Sampson made herself a suit of men's clothes and signed up for the army, pretending to be a man named Robert Shurtleff. She fooled everyone for the three years that she fought alongside the men. Though she was wounded twice, she still volunteered for dangerous assignments. When she became sick and nearly died, the doctor treating her learned her secret. She had to leave the army then, but after the war was over Deborah received soldier's retirement pay. She was an example, said the Congress, "of female heroism, fidelity, and courage."

SPY

When British officers decided to use Lydia Darragh's house in Philadelphia as their headquarters, she listened in on them, then wrote what they said in code, and sewed the messages behind the buttons of the coat her son wore to visit his brother in the army. One night Lydia heard the enemy plotting a surprise attack on Washington's camp. She made up an excuse to leave the city and walked until she found a soldier who could get the information to the American army in time.

GUNNER

After John Corbin was killed at Fort Washington, New York, his wife, Margaret, took over his artillery position. By the time the British won the battle, she had received three gunshot wounds, but Margaret never stopped firing. Her wounds made it impossible for her to work, so Congress gave her the same money as other disabled soldiers. She is buried at the military academy at West Point.

MESSENGER

The British captured eighteen-year-old Emily Geiger as she carried a secret message from General Greene through enemy territory on horseback. The soldiers called in a woman to search her, giving Emily time to memorize and swallow the note. When she was set free, despite the danger, she continued on and delivered the important information.

HOME-FRONT PATRIOT

A huge British force was set to destroy a small American army unit as it pulled out of New York in defeat. But the generals stopped for dinner at a home along the way. There Mary Murray gave them so much to drink that the Americans were able to escape without the British knowing about it, and Mrs. Murray was given the credit for saving that part of the American army.

Esther DeBerdt Reed

E. Reed

As an intelligent English teenager interested in the world around her, Esther DeBerdt fell in love with Joseph Reed, a smart young American studying law in London. After five years, the couple finally married and moved to America.

From Philadelphia, Esther wrote to her brother of the growing unhappiness in the American colonies and soon she was siding with her new country against the British. When Joseph went off to war and she had to move around from place to place with her tiny children to avoid the enemy, Esther declared that she was willing to give up the money from her husband's business and put up with him being away so long because "I think the cause in which he is engaged so just, so glorious, and I hope so victorious." She had become a true American woman.

That's what she called herself when she published what has become a famous newspaper article: "Sentiments of an American Woman." In it she appealed to the women of the country to support the troops who were suffering from lack of clothes, food, and housing. Even though she had just given birth to her sixth baby, Esther organized a fund-raising drive in Philadelphia, where women went door to door asking for money for the soldiers. Women all around the country soon copied her efforts, and before long they raised more than $300,000 and made a huge difference in troop morale.

W HEN Esther published "Sentiments of an American Woman," it was a low point in the war. The British looked like they were winning, and conditions for American soldiers were terrible. Esther wanted to assure the men that they were not forgotten: "Forgotten! never; I can answer in the name of all my sex. Brave Americans, your disinterestedness, your courage, and your constancy will always be dear to America, as long as she shall preserve her virtue."

Esther wanted the money she raised to buy something for the troops that they wouldn't have otherwise, something special. General Washington demanded the women use the cash to buy linen for shirts. The two argued back and forth in letters, but Washington eventually won. The women made more than two thousand shirts, but they made them special by sewing their own names on them so every soldier knew his shirt came from a woman who cared about him and about the cause he was fighting for.

SARAH LIVINGSTON JAY

Sarah Jay

ONE OF FIVE FEISTY DAUGHTERS OF NEW JERSEY governor William Livingston, Sarah, called Sally, charmed the young men of New York when she went for a visit as a teenager. A family friend wrote to Sally's sister after a party that he saw one lovesick gentleman "rolling up his eyes and sighing most piteously" and another with "his shoulders drawn up to his ears." The next year eighteen-year-old Sally married a thirty-year-old lawyer by the name of John Jay.

John went into politics, serving in the Continental Congress in Philadelphia while Sally was left to move with her baby boy from place to place to avoid the British. She always managed to keep her sense of humor in the steady stream of letters she wrote home to her parents and sisters. In the middle of one letter, a doctor walked into her house announcing bad news. "Aye, Doctor, what now?" When he told her the British were nearby, Sally joked: "Wherever I am, I think there are alarms."

John Jay was elected president of the Continental Congress and then appointed as ambassador to Spain. Sally went with him across the ocean, first to Spain and then to France, where she became a good friend of Benjamin Franklin and was so beautiful she was mistaken for the French queen. When the Jays returned to America with their two little girls born abroad, it was the first time Sally had seen her little boy in five years!

THE ship taking Sally and John to Spain hit stormy waters after a couple of weeks at sea. First the masts broke and then the rudder, so the captain decided to sail to Martinique to find a different ship. That ship took two months to reach Europe! When the Jays finally were ready to dock in Spain, a British ship started chasing them, trying to capture the American Patriots. But they made it safely to harbor in Cadiz.

The trip by land from Cadiz to Madrid was almost as bad as the sea voyage, and Sally was expecting a baby. One night the couple stayed in an inn, only to discover that the room next to them had been "allotted to our mules." The animals were wearing bells and didn't sleep much, so the Jays found themselves "serenaded with the tinkling" all night long.

CATHARINE LITTLEFIELD GREENE

Caty Greene

MARTHA WASHINGTON WASN'T THE ONLY GENERAL'S WIFE IN THE military camps; several others also spent their winters with the troops. General Nathanael Greene was a volunteer soldier in Rhode Island when he rushed to sign up with Washington's army at the beginning of the war. Soon his new young bride joined him.

Catharine Littlefield was born on Block Island, where women actually wore pants to ride horses! (No women *ever* wore pants then.) But after her mother died, she lived with her aunt on the Rhode Island mainland, where she met and married Nathanael when she was nineteen years old. She hated staying home without her husband and traveled to meet him whenever she could, even though she had a baby almost every year. One of the babies was even born at camp!

The baby cheered everyone up, and so did Caty (or Kitty—different people called her different nicknames). She organized parties and dances and one time danced with George Washington for three hours straight without sitting down!

By the time the war was over, the Greenes had five children and no

money. They moved to Georgia, where Nathanael soon died. President George Washington honored Caty by visiting the plantation that she was working hard to make successful. She also fought with Congress to pay her back the money Nathanael had spent to clothe his troops, and eventually Congress passed a law giving her the funds. Her old friend the president was happy to sign the law.

CATY loved to tell a story about what happened to Nathanael one night when he was in charge of the southern military command. After losing a battle, the general and the governor of South Carolina found one bed for the two of them. Each accused the other of kicking. It turned out that a hog was in the bed!

Eli Whitney worked on Caty's plantation as a toolmaker and heard the Georgia planters complain about how hard it was to remove seeds from cotton. He built a laboratory in the house and there invented the cotton gin, which made it fifty times faster to remove the seeds from cotton, so much more cotton could be harvested and sold. Some people think Caty helped Whitney invent the cotton gin or even that he stole the idea from her. She certainly gave him the money to manufacture the invention, and then she shared in the money when it was patented.

DOLLEY MADISON

D. P. Madison

"QUEEN DOLLEY," SHE WAS CALLED, AND IN FACT Dolley Madison reigned over Washington for a very long time, especially in her eight years as First Lady. "Everybody loves Mrs. Madison," Congressman Henry Clay told her.

Dolley came to Washington as the wife of the secretary of state. She met Congressman James Madison in Philadelphia when she was a young widow with a small son. Her first husband and baby had died in a yellow fever epidemic that swept the city. She married James, though he was seventeen years older and not of her Quaker religion, and moved to Montpelier, the Madison home in Virginia.

Then it was on to Washington, where Dolley gave nonstop parties for all the politicians, and when her husband was elected president, Dolley got a lot of the credit for his victory. She was so powerful that people asked her to get them jobs with the government.

During the War of 1812, she showed great courage as the British invaded Washington. She barely escaped with her life and then came back after just a couple of days to help rebuild the burned-out city.

Dolley's bravery earned her praise among the people and in the press. When Madison left office and the couple retired to Virginia, everyone was distressed to see Dolley depart. Here's how one newspaper said good-bye: "Like a summer's sun she rose in our political horizon, gloriously."

The City of Washington, the Capital of the United States of America was taken

the White House

"I am still here within the sound of the cannon!" Dolley wrote to her sister as the British stormed into Washington. President Madison was away visiting the troops, leaving her home alone in the White House. She tried to wait for her husband to return from the battlefield, but her friends insisted she find a safer place. Dolley wouldn't budge "until the large picture of General Washington is secured." She didn't want the British to destroy the portrait of the first president and dishonor Washington. When the enemy troops arrived at the empty White House, they sat down and ate the dinner Dolley had prepared.

The war left many children without fathers, so Dolley worked with the other women in Washington to set up the Female Orphan Asylum. She became its "First Directress" and helped not only to provide a place for the girls to live but also to receive an education and get work. Women all over the country were beginning to see that orphans and other poor people were in need, and they started institutions to help them.

$\mathcal{C}$onclusion

"The women here are taking a station in society which is not known elsewhere," wrote journalist Margaret Bayard Smith after she had lived in Washington for several years. She rejoiced in the fact that the new Capital City was a place where women were taken seriously "in the court, in the representative hall, as well as in the drawing room." America was a new country, trying out a new form of government, and even though it would be more than a hundred years from the time Margaret wrote those words before women could vote, the men were already hearing women's voices talking about the important issues of the day. And the men we call the Founding Fathers listened.

From the time before the Revolution when women were called on to resist the British, through the war where some clashed on the battlefront and some cared for their families on the home front, through the formation of the government, women had shown how important they were to the new country.

George Washington wrote to Patriot poet Annis Boudinot Stockton at the end of the Revolution: "You ladies are in the number of the best Patriots America can boast." The Father of the Country knew America would not have become a nation without its Founding Mothers.

# $\mathcal{A}$cknowledgments

No BOOK, especially not a beautiful book like this, ever happens as the result of one person's effort. Diane Goode is not only a truly inspired artist; her appreciation of this distaff history informs these delightful and detailed depictions of the women and their work.

Diane has thanked the team at HarperCollins Children's, and I want to second her sentiments. But before there was this book, there was the "grown-up" book, *Founding Mothers: The Women Who Raised Our Nation*. It would not have happened without Claire Wachtel, editor and coconspirator in telling the stories of the other half of the human race—women. I turned to my longtime friend Ann Charnley to diligently dig up elusive information about these difficult-to-document heroines. She in turn was helped by:

The great Jim Billington, who introduced us to the Library of Congress's Manuscript and Women's Studies Divisions.

Holly C. Schulman at the University of Virginia, where she edits the remarkable Dolley Madison Digital Edition.

Plus the Huntington Library, the South Caroliniana Library at the University of South Carolina, and the Butler Library at Columbia University, along with the historical societies of Massachusetts, South Carolina, Pennsylvania, New York, New Jersey, and Virginia. Add to those the Mount Vernon Ladies' Association, the John Jay Homestead, and the Schuyler Mansion.

When Diane decided that she wanted to draw the actual signatures of the ladies whose stories are here, we went back to our friends at those institutions plus a couple of others. Special thanks to Henry Fulmer at South Caroliniana, Tammy Kiter at the New-York Historical Society, Elaine Grubin at the Massachusetts Historical Society, and Janet Bloom at the University of Michigan's Clements Library. Diane did such a precise job copying the signatures she could start a new career as counterfeiter.

Finally, a thank-you to my family. This book was originally my husband Steven's idea, and he has cheered me on through it as he has through most of my life. Our six grandchildren made particularly helpful suggestions. And they love Diane's work almost as much as I do.

Cokie Roberts

WITH SINCERE GRATITUDE to Cokie Roberts for her spirited and generous support from start to finish. To my agent, Steve Malk, and to our very talented team—Maria Modugno, Martha Rago, Dana Fritts, Annie Stone, and Alyson Day—thank you for understanding my passion for the subject and allowing me the freedom to follow my artistic vision. And David, my love, thank you for finding the beautiful antique pens and inkwells; each time the nib caught on and splattered the paper, as it would have done in the eighteenth century, I was brought closer in spirit to our Founding Mothers.

In addition, I gratefully acknowledge the following academic institutions for use of original signatures as the basis for handwritten facsimiles: William L. Clements Library; Massachusetts Historical Society; New-York Historical Society; Yale University Library; South Caroliniana Library, University of South Carolina; Columbia University Rare Book & Manuscript Library; and the Rhode Island Historical Society.

Diane Goode

FIND OUT MORE ABOUT THE FOUNDING MOTHERS

The Library of Congress, American Women
http://memory.loc.gov/ammem/awhhtml/index.html

Massachusetts Historical Society, Correspondence between John and Abigail Adams
http://www.masshist.org/digitaladams/aea/index.html

The White House
http://www.whitehouse.gov/

First Ladies
www.whitehouse.gov/about/first-ladies

National Archives
http://www.archives.gov/exhibits/charters/charters.html

Abigail Adams
http://www.abigailadams.org/

Dolley Madison
www.pbs.org/wgbh/americanexperience/films/dolley/

Eliza Lucas Pinckney
www.distinguishedwomen.com/biographies/pinckney.html

Mercy Otis Warren
http://www.masshist.org/bh/mercybio.html

Martha Washington
http://www.ushistory.org/valleyforge/served/martha.html

Phillis Wheatley
www.poetryfoundation.org/bio/phillis-wheatley

This book supports the Common Core Learning Standards for English Language Arts & Literacy in History/Social Studies.

THE SENTIMENTS of an
AMERICAN WOMAN.

ON the commencement of actual war, the Women of America manifested a firm reso-
lution to contribute as much as could depend on them, to the deliverance of their country. Animated by the purest patriotism, they are sensible of sorrow at this day, In not offer-
ing more than barren wishes for the success of so glorious a Revolution. They aspire to ren-
der themselves more really useful; and this sentiment is universal from the north to the south
of the Thirteen United States. Our ambition is kindled by the fame of those heroines of an-
tiquity, who have rendered their sex illustrious, and have proved to the universe, that, if
the weakness of our Constitution, if opinion s d or bid to mo to glo-
ry by the same paths as the we should and em in our
love for the public good. I g all that we sex has mendable.
I call to mind with enthusiasm with ad n, all tho e of constancy and patriotism, which hist has trans The pe oured by Heaven,
preferved from destruction by virtues resolu of Deborah of Judah,
of Esther! The fortitude of ther o g up her sons to die before her eyes: Rome saved from y the efforts of Volumnia,
and other Roman Ladies: So s t the Women have been seen forget-
ting the weakness of their sex, buildin new trenches with their feeble hands,
furnishing arms to their defenders, they them the missile weapons on the enemy, resigning the ornaments of their appar me, to fill the public treasury
and to hasten the deliverance of their count ves under it's ruins, throwing
themselves into the flames rather than f humiliation before a proud
enemy.

LIBERTY

Born for liberty, disdaining to bear the Government, we associate ourselves to the grandeur of those Sovereig who have held with so much
splendour the scepter of the greatest State zabeths, the Maries, the Ca-
tharines, who have extended the empire d to reign by sweetness and
justice, have broken the chains of sla the times of ignorance and
barbarity. The Spanish Women, do they the most patriotic sacrifices,
to encrease the means of victory in the He is a friend to the French
Nation. They are our allies. We call d, that it was a French Maid
who kindled up amongst her fellow-cit tism buried under long mis-
fortunes: It was the Maid of Orleans gdom of France the ancestors
of those same British, whose odious yoke off; and whom it is necessary
that we drive from this Continent.

But I must limit myself to the re coll- ber of atchievements. Who
knows if persons disposed to censure with regard to us, may not
disapprove our appearing ac quai our sex boasts? We are
at least certain, that he no citizen who will not ap ours for the relief
of the armies which nd , our possessions, our liberty? I of our soldiery
has been represented evils inseparable from war, and the firm generous spirit
which has enabled them support these. But it has been said, that they may apprehend, that
in the course of a long war, the view of their distresses may be lost, and their services be forgotten. Forgotten! never; I can answer in the name of all my sex. Brave Americans, your
disinterestedness, your courage, and your constancy will always be dear to America, as long
as she shall preserve her virtue.
We know that at a distance from the theatre of war, if we enjoy any tranquility, it is the
fruit of your watchings, your labours, your dangers. If I live happy in the midst of my family;